THE PROCESS OF GRAPHIC DESIGN AS ILLUSTRATED

THROUGH THE PROJECT BREAD + MILK + EGGS

by

Bryson Currier

An Honors thesis submitted to the Department of Art in partial fulfillment of the

requirements for the degree of Bachelor of Arts

Meredith College

Raleigh, North Carolina

May 9, 2019

Publication Agreement

I hereby grant to Meredith College the non-exclusive right to reproduce, and/or distribute this work in whole or in part worldwide, in any format or medium for non-commercial, academic purposes only. Readers of this work have the right to use it for non-commercial, academic purposes as defined by the "fair use" doctrine of U.S. copyright law, so long as all attributions and copyright statements are retained. Meredith College may keep more than one copy of this submission for purposes of security, backup and preservation.

Bryson Currier | May 9, 2019

OVERVIEW

For my senior thesis I completed a project that required me to propose a company, complete with a design brief, that would demand a full suite of graphic design materials. Following this proposal that fleshed out the company, its target audience, and the individual tiers of design projects that it would require, I had to complete those design projects. The company that I came up with was a vending machine-style convenience store called *BREAD + MILK + EGGS* that provided staples such as bread, milk and eggs by way of many conveniently located stores. The target audience was young to middle aged adults living in large housing developments, outside of which these stores would be located. The four tiers of design that *BREAD + MILK + EGGS* required were a logo that established a set of brand-standards by which all of the other design components drew influence, a series of package designs, various forms of advertisements, and a fully developed phone application. Throughout the semester, I kept a process book that included every step of the project from beginning to end and submitted it for a grade. Finally, I had to present each finalized tier in the format of a presentation board that followed my company's brand standards.

THE DESIGN BRIEF

My design brief was completed to establish the end goals and trajectory of the entire semester-long project, as well as to provide a source of formal practice of design brief development as is standard in the design industry. When a designer is working with a client, he or she is expected to produce a design brief in a project's genesis, outlining the objectives of the project along with every step of the design process that will be made. This insures that there is no grey area between the designer and client and that all that is entailed in the design undertaking is clear to both parties before any work on the project begins. My design brief for *BREAD + MILK + EGGS* was simple. It described the company that I wanted to create, establishing a target audience, company philosophy, project summary, and outlined the various tiers of the project that would be developed in full design process; this design process always includes research, sketches, computer roughs, various rounds of critique, finalization and presentation. The following is my comprehensive design brief for *BREAD + MILK + EGGS* as it appeared in my process book.

Project Title

BREAD + MILK + EGGS

Location

Entrances to major housing developments

First store: 5433 Wade Park Blvd #132, Raleigh, NC 27607

Market

All residents of nearby housing developments (predominantly young to middle aged)

Project Abstract

BREAD + MILK + EGGS is a friendly neighborhood store nestled just outside of or within large housing developments. It is the desire of BREAD + MILK + EGGS to provide families with the lastminute essentials that are so often in short supply, making trips to the grocery store less frequent. The purpose of BREAD +

MILK + EGGS is to make life better by providing easy access to the kitchen staples you need, whenever you need them.

Project Description

BREAD + MILK + EGGS is a company founded on convenience and simplicity. The store fronts are all open at all times to ensure that no one goes without an ingredient they need. It provides user friendly vending, functioning without an attendant. All of the product packaging is plastic free and recyclable, ensuring that BREAD + MILK + EGGS is not a drain on the environment. The products are sourced from our pre-approved farmers who ensure the most upstanding treatment of their animals. BREAD + MILK + EGGS provides more than bread, milk, and eggs, including popular herbs, butter, and a variety of meats, as well as some fruits and vegetables. Also available for purchase are prepackaged meals that contain every ingredient needed to cook them, as well as easy to use instructions. BREAD + MILK + EGGS is a population-based company that plants its store fronts just outside of dense housing developments that are more than five minutes away from the nearest grocery store, giving the families of the development convenient access to the things they are most likely to need. Because BREAD + MILK + EGGS can function without an attendant and directly sources its produce, the price of the products is comparable to, if not less than what one would pay in a standard grocery store for the same product.

Project Statement

My design solution for BREAD + MILK + EGGS is to create an eye-catching brand that represents the ease of form and function that BREAD + MILK

+ EGGS is seeking to bring their consumers. I am going to simplify every part of the design to just the essentials, mirroring the ease with which one can acquire their products. I will use a simple type lockup or icons for the logo and intend to keep the design entirely black and white, save one bold accent color. I will use a sanserif font or font pairing and will keep the use of type to a minimum. I do not intend to use imagery, only clean, bold type.

Design Speculation

   Tier One: Identity Design

   -   Logo that establishes brand standards

   Tier Two: Package Design

   -   Milk Packaging

   -   Bread Packaging

   -   Eggs Packaging

   Tier Three: Promotion

   -   Billboard advertisement

   -   Series of print advertisements

   -   Series of banner advertisements

   Tier Four: Application Design

   -   Fully developed phone application

THE RESEARCH

The project as a whole began with research to explore the market for a company like *BREAD + MILK + EGGS*, as well as to document visual inspiration for the brand style that I wanted to develop. As a designer it is important that I do visual research, not only to gain excitement and knowledge about how to design successfully for the project's objectives, but also to insure originality in design. Much like in the laws of driving, ignorance is no excuse in design. A designer must do research to educate him or herself on the graphic design that has already been created in order to prevent visual plagiarism in their designs. In addition to my initial research, each tier of the project required its own research to develop a final product that complied with industry standards and felt new and exciting. In the pursuit of sources from which to draw visual inspiration, I used creative platforms of social media such as *Pinterest* and *Bēhance*. These are excellent sources of design inspiration because they are always up to date and have millions of contributors worldwide. I also looked to individual companies that I admired, such as *BRANDLESS* and *Cava,* for inspiration. The research for each tier was documented by way of printed images of inspirational design work that fit into the same category as the designated tier; these prints were organized together in the process book that housed all of the work on the project.

TIER DEVELOPMENT & PROJECT EXECUTION

The development of each of the four tiers followed a path that is typical of graphic design projects. As previously stated, the design process includes research, sketches, computer roughs, various rounds of critique, finalization and presentation. I have already established my undertaking of the research component and will now breakdown the other steps of the design process through the lens of this project.

The sketching component is the next phase following visual research documentation. In the sketching of thumbnails, which are small sketches that outline the basic elements of a potential design solution, a designer applies his or her research in the illustration of new ideas for the overall look of the final product. While making thumbnails, a designer's objective is to translate onto paper what he or she is seeing and calculating as a design solution. Thumbnails and larger sketches force the designer into full exploration of design solutions and often result in new ideas and solutions that the designer had not previously thought of. When sketching thumbnails for the logo component of *BREAD + MILK + EGGS,* I discovered that my original intention to have the logo be either solely a typographic lockup or a cluster of icons was not what I wanted. I decided that the logo would best represent *BREAD + MILK + EGGS* if it had both type and icons in tandem, thus eliminating potential consumer confusion. I wanted to stick to the simplicity that the company stood for as outlined in the design brief and I decided that I could still achieve this in a logo that had both icons and a typographic lockup if I simplified the icons as much as possible.

The next stage of the process that follows sketching is taking the sketches to the computer and developing computer roughs. There are different approaches to this part of the process. With some designs it is easiest to take and upload a photograph of your sketch into the *Adobe* program in which you intend to execute the design and proceed to build on top of the photographed sketch. Other designs can be roughed out in the program with the designer using their sketch as a visual reference for direction. Tier one, like most logo development, used the first method; the other three tiers used the latter. Working on top of and off of my sketches, I developed computer roughs of my design ideas for each tier of the project that gave better life to the design solutions I had concocted for *BREAD + MILK + EGGS*. In the stage of computer roughs there is still much exploration of innovative design executions and color combinations. Just as in the rest of the design stages, when working on computer roughs a designer would be remiss in discarding any work because it illustrates how their time has been spent and may be of importance down the road.

Critique is essential to a successful result in the design process because it subjects the design solutions to outside opinions. When working for a client, a designer will likely be working within a creative team or in the vicinity of other designers, providing many opportunities for group critique or individual feedback. When working on a design, it is easy to become enveloped in the project and overcommitted to an idea. The eyes of others who have not been involved in the designer's process are fresh and offer a new perspective and unbiased impression of the work. Some rounds of critique involve client feedback that can guide a designer closer to a successful solution, while simultaneously allowing the client to have an updated say in the overall direction. Throughout the course of this project, I was my own client and looked forward to group critique to provide alternate perspectives to my own. Each tier of the project was subject to group critiques or individual feedback that greatly improved my designs. Whether it was choosing the strongest color ratio or the suggestion of a hybrid of two layout concepts, the opinions of other designers helped me push my work even further.

Finalization of a design involves tying up any loose ends such as smoothing rough curves in vector graphics or meeting a client to present them with slightly varying and nearly complete design concepts. Finalization is all of the easier portions of the process that require much less time and labor. For *BREAD + MILK + EGGS*, each tier experienced a period of finalization in which it was subject to a concluding critique and last round of edits.

After finalization comes presentation. All design projects conclude with presentation to the client and the relinquishing of the files upon payment by the client. For each tier of *BREAD + MILK + EGGS,* I had to submit final design files and complete presentation boards. Presentation boards are printed layouts that showcase the final design for the project. They are formatted within the brand standards established by the project and mockup the graphic design element in a way that is realistic to its function. Tier one's presentation board showed the finalized *BREAD + MILK + EGGS* logo in all of its various formats and gave a brief project overview alongside my color swatches and typefaces. For tiers two through four, my presentation boards featured images rendered in *Adobe Photoshop*, making it look as though my designs for *BREAD + MILK + EGGS* had already been printed and photographed. When presenting to a client, presentation boards such as these can be used to show them exactly how your finished design should be used and will look as it functions. My presentation boards were submitted alongside my process book that illustrated every step that led me to these completed design elements.

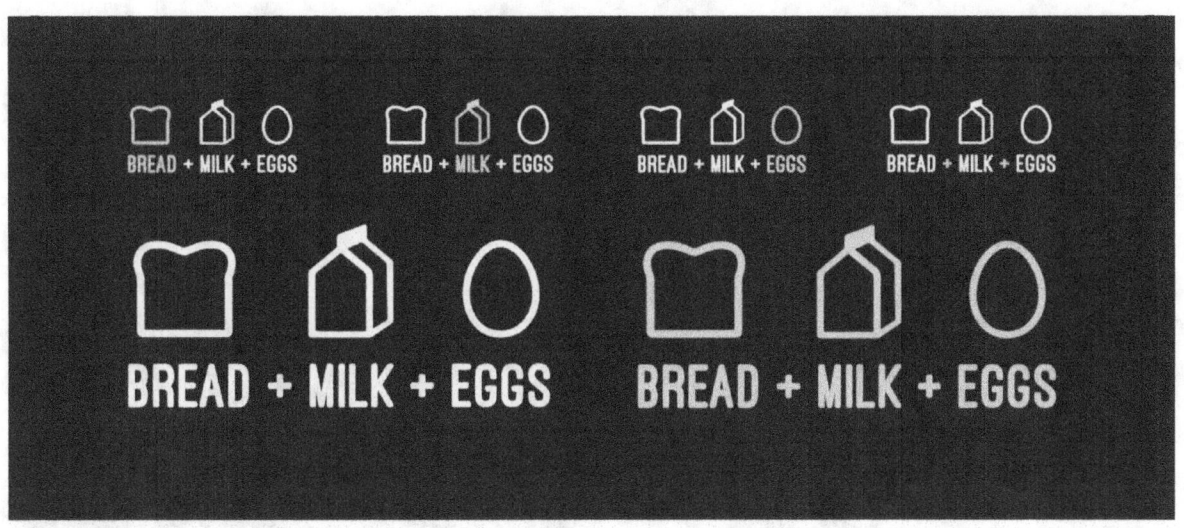

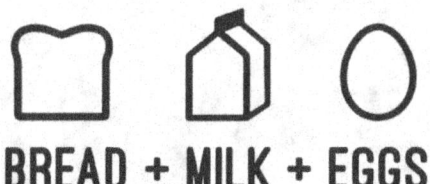

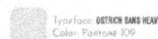

IDENTITY DESIGN
The Senior Project is the culminating project in a designer's academic career, and it should provide an answer to an intellectual question in an original and thorough manner.

BREAD + MILK + EGGS is a convenience store that is just that: convenient. It is open 24/7 and provides the products most often in short supply, so that you don't have to drive to the grocery store every time you run out of a household staple. In addition to making your life more efficient, **BREAD + MILK + EGGS** uses all recyclable, plastic-free packaging and provides a rewards program for returned glass bottles.

Typeface: **OSTRICH SANS HEAVY**
Color: Pantone 309

PRESENTATION BOARD TIER ONE

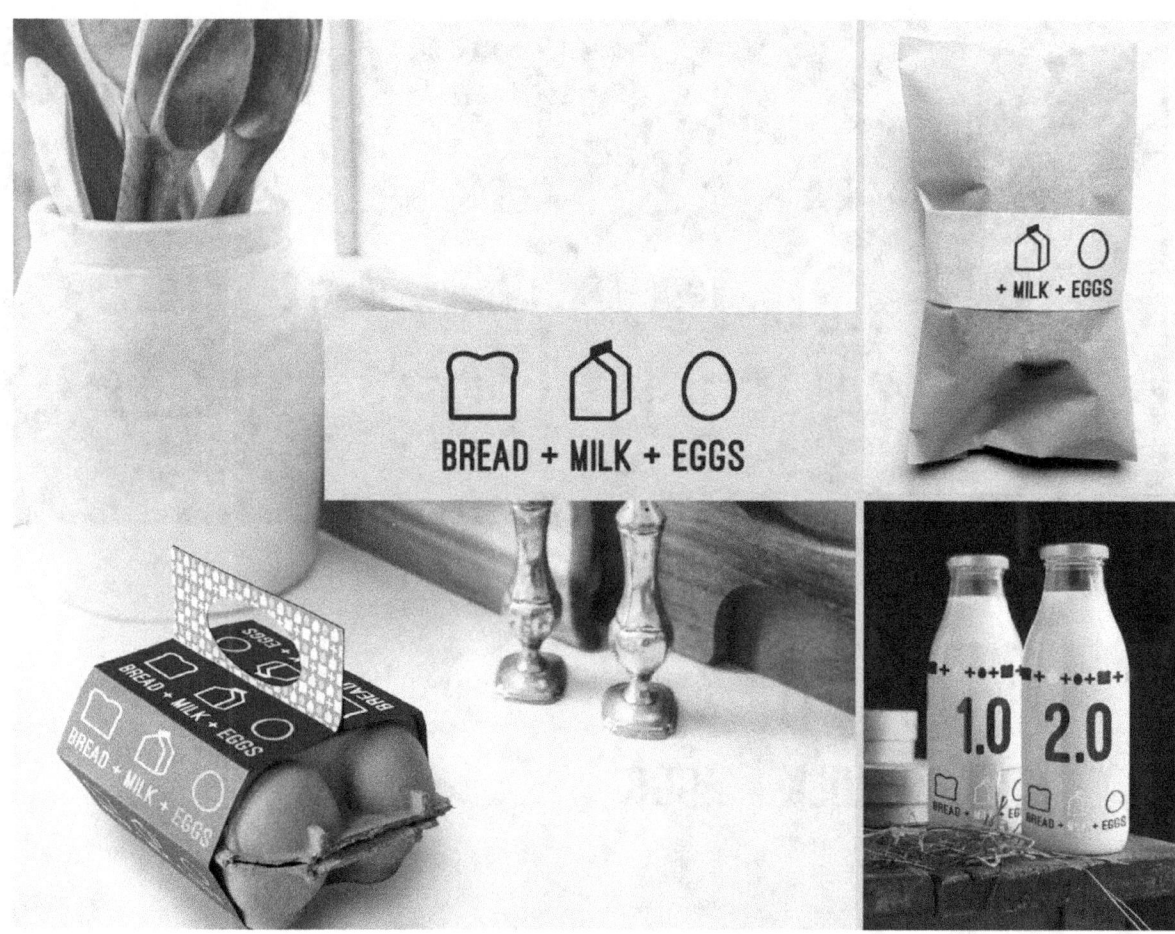

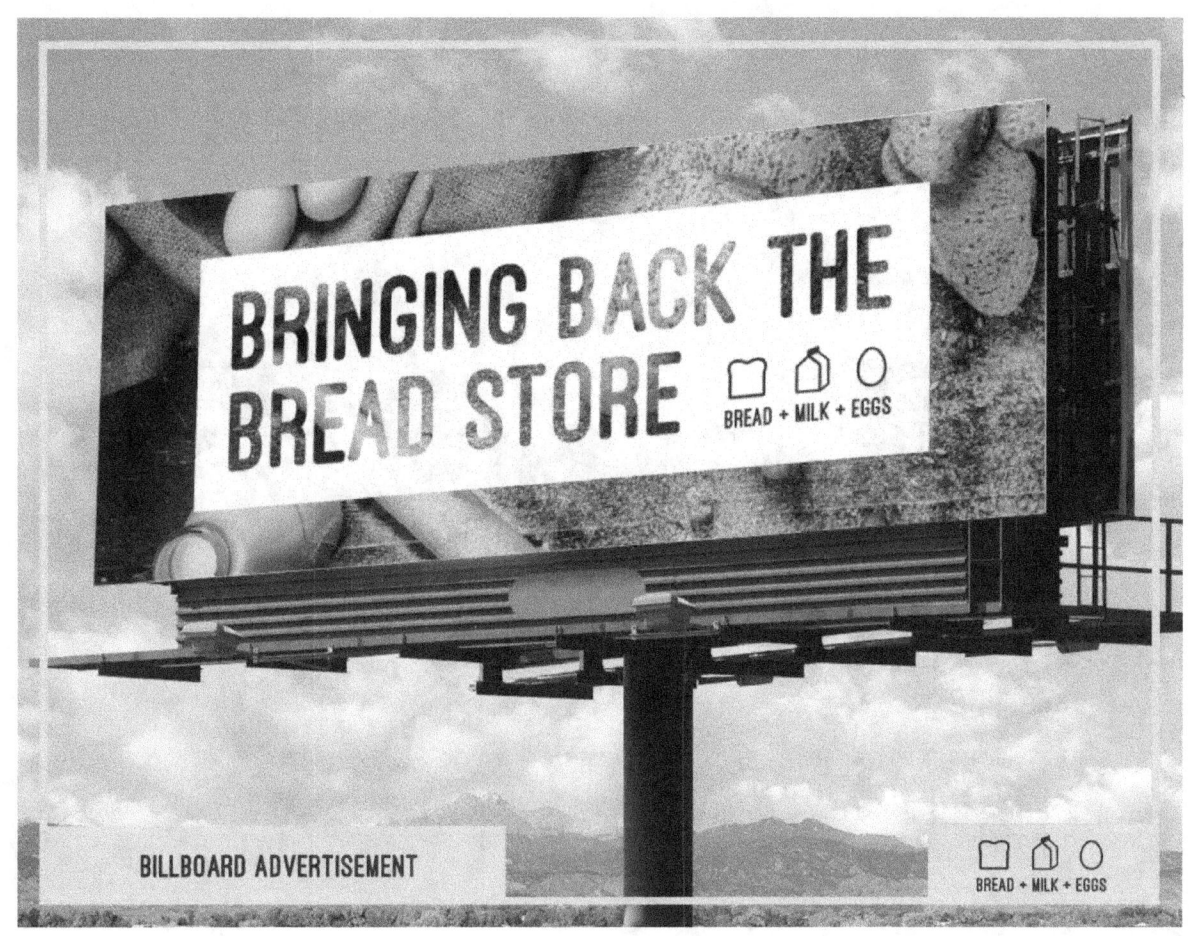

PRESENTATION BOARD TIER THREE

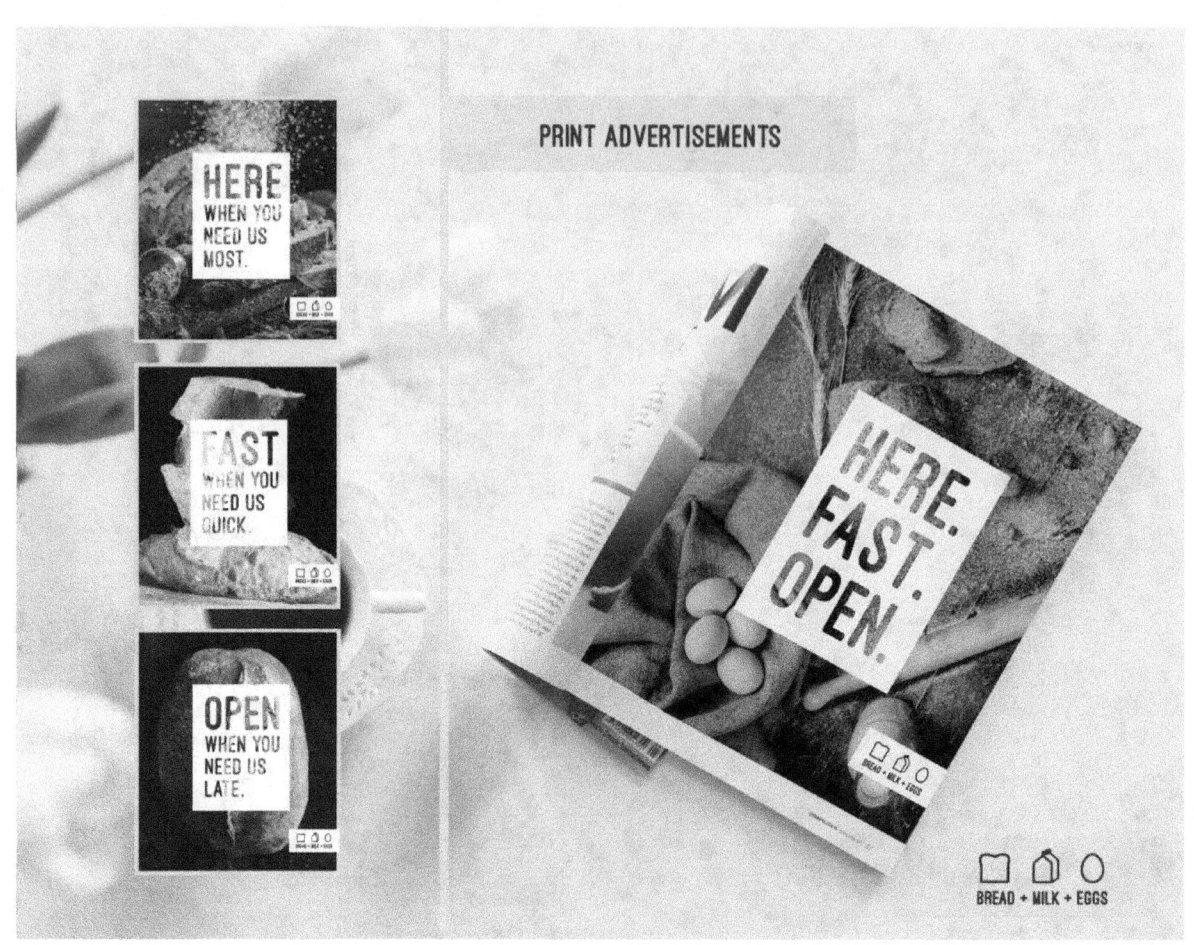

PRESENTATION BOARD TIER THREE

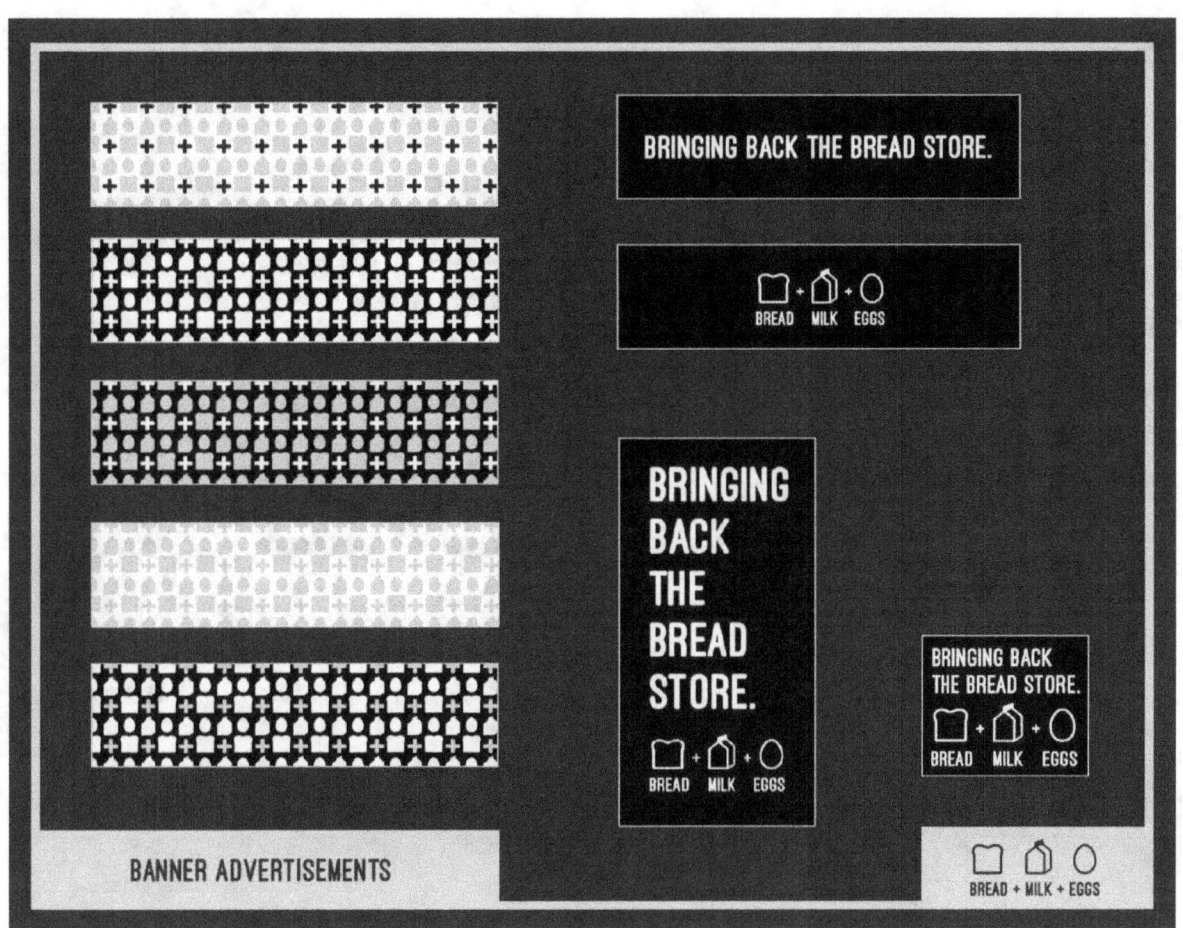

PRESENTATION BOARD TIER THREE

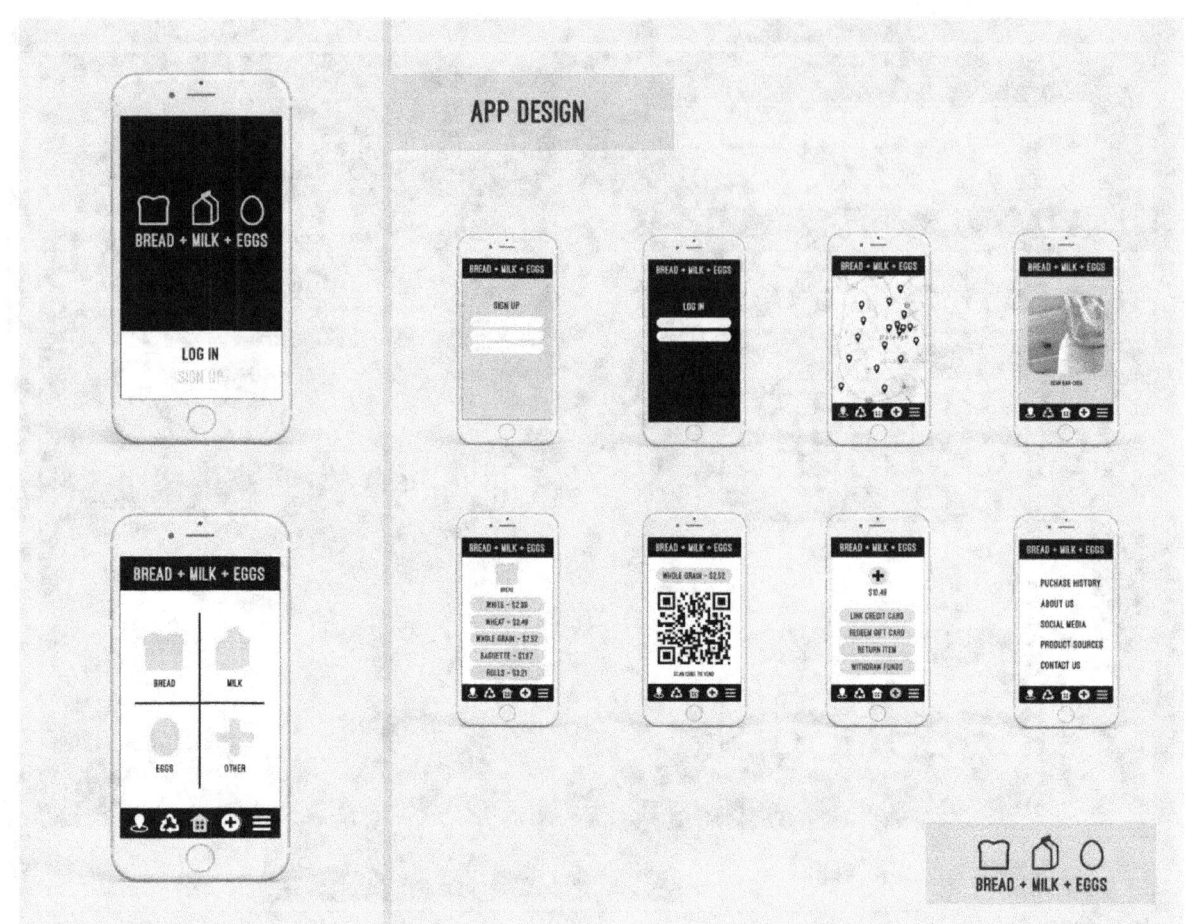

APP DESIGN

PRESENTATION BOARD TIER FOUR

WORKS CITED

Behance. "Top Creative Work On Behance." *Behance*, www.behance.net/.

"Better Stuff. Fewer Dollars. It's That Simple." *Brandless*, brandless.com/.

CAVA, cava.com/.

Crawford, Tad. *AIGA Professional Practices in Graphic Design*. Skyhorse Publishing,
    Inc., 2010.

Crawford, Tad. *The Graphic Design Business Book*. Allworth, 2006.

Fawcett-Tang, Roger, and Daniel Mason. *Experimental Formats & Packaging: Creative
    Solutions for Inspiring Graphic Design*. RotoVision, 2007.

Hamlin, Robert P. "The Consumer Testing of Food Package Graphic Design." *British
    Food Journal*, vol. 118, no. 2, 2016, pp. 379–395., doi:10.1108/bfj-03-2015-0105.

"Pinterest." *Pinterest*, www.pinterest.com/.

Skolos, Nancy, and Thomas Wedell. *Type, Image, Message: Merging Pictures and Ideas:
    a Graphic Design Layout Workshop*. Rockport Publishers, 2006.

Thompson, Bradbury. *Art of Graphic Design*. Yale University Press, 2018.

White, Alex. *The Elements of Graphic Design*. Allworth, 2011.

[This page intentionally left blank.]

[This page intentionally left blank.]

[This page intentionally left blank.]

[This page intentionally left blank.]

[This page intentionally left blank.]

[This page intentionally left blank.]

[This page intentionally left blank.]

[This page intentionally left blank.]

[This page intentionally left blank.]

[This page intentionally left blank.]

[This page intentionally left blank.]

[This page intentionally left blank.]

[This page intentionally left blank.]

[This page intentionally left blank.]

[This page intentionally left blank.]